W9-BSD-571

SEASONS
SPRING

Stephanie Turnbull

Published by Smart Apple Media
P.O. Box 1329
Mankato, MN 56002

Printed in the United States of America,
at Corporate Graphics in North Mankato, Minnesota.

Designed by Hel James
Edited by Mary-Jane Wilkins

Library of Congress Cataloging-in-Publication Data

Turnbull, Stephanie.
  Spring / by Stephanie Turnbull.
     p. cm. -- (The seasons)
  Includes index.
  Summary: "Uses photos to help describe the changes
that happen to the weather, plants, and animals in
spring. Mentions the holidays and events that usually
occur in spring months"--Provided by publisher.
  Audience: Grades K-3.
  ISBN 978-1-59920-847-3 (hbk. : library bound)
  1. Spring--Juvenile literature. I. Title.
  QB637.5.T87 2013
  508.2--dc23

Photo acknowledgements
t = top, b = bottom, l = left, r = right, c = center
page 1 DenisNata/Shutterstock; 3 iStockphoto/
Thinkstock; 5 majeczka/Shutterstock; 6 Hallgerd/
Shutterstock; 7 Ryan McVay/Thinkstock;
8 Anest/Shutterstock; 9 Smileus/Shutterstock;
10 Vishnevskiy Vasily/Shutterstock; 11t&b
iStockphoto/Thinkstock; 12b clearviewstock/
Shutterstock; 13 t&b iStockphoto/Thinkstock;
14 iStockphoto/Thinkstock; 15 visuelldesign/
Shutterstock; 16t iStockphoto/Thinkstock,
b AlessandroZocc/Shutterstock; 17 Steshkin
Yevgeniy/Shutterstock; 18b iStockphoto/Thinkstock,
c Hemera/Thinkstock; 19 Cynthia Kidwell/
Shutterstock; 20 DenisNata/Shutterstock;
21 Jenny Mie Lau King/Shutterstock; 22 t&b
3 iStockphoto/Thinkstock; 23l iStockphoto/
Thinkstock, b Hemera/Thinkstock, r Dirk Ott/
Shutterstock
Cover iStockphoto/Thinkstock

DAD0505
042012
9 8 7 6 5 4 3 2 1

Contents

It's Spring!

Bright flowers push up
through melting snow.

Sunny Spring

Our spring months are March, April and May.

The sun comes up earlier every morning and sets later every evening.

Days are lighter and warmer.

Nature comes back to life after winter.

Windy Weather

It is often windy in spring. This makes the weather change quickly.

One minute it is bright and breezy…

… the next minute
it is pouring
with rain!

Look for a **rainbow**
when sun shines on rain.

Time to Grow

Warm spring sun and rain help new plants sprout from the soil.

Leaf buds on tree branches uncurl and *s p r e a d*.

Masses of white and pink flowers called blossom open on fruit trees.

Finding Food

In spring, many birds fly back
from winter homes further south.
Animals wake from a long, cozy sleep.

Everyone
is hungry!

Busy bees collect
sweet nectar
from flowers.

Wiggling
worms make
tasty meals
for birds.

Here I Am!

Spring can be NOISY.
Animals call and sing
to each other.

Frogs puff out their
throats to make
deep croaks.

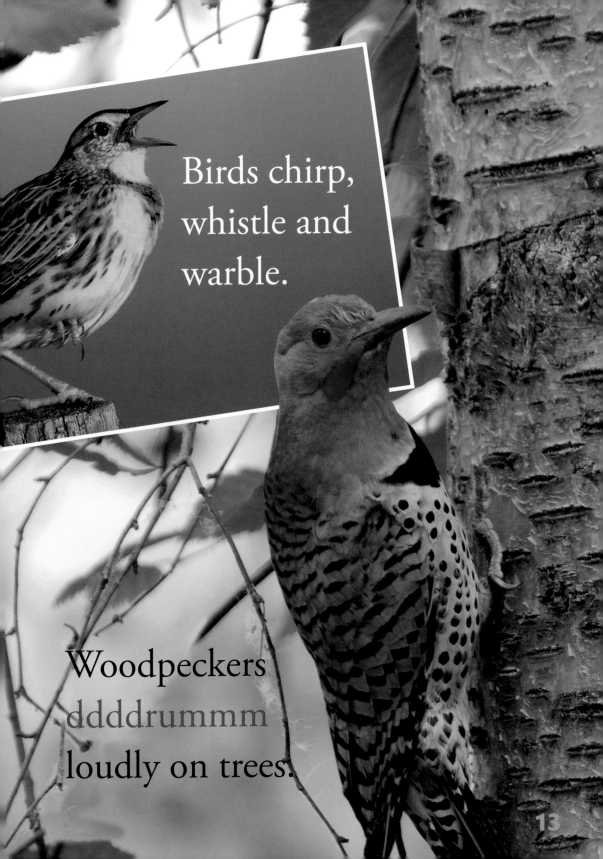

Birds chirp, whistle and warble.

Woodpeckers ddddrummm loudly on trees.

Busy Builders

Animals are soon busy making nests for babies.

Birds build nests from twigs, leaves, grass, and mud.

Wasps turn
soggy bits
of wood into
papery tubes.

Eggs Everywhere

Birds lay just a few eggs...

...but some animals lay hundreds! These are tiny butterfly eggs.

16

Birds keep their eggs safe
and warm until…CRACK!

Babies break out of their shells.

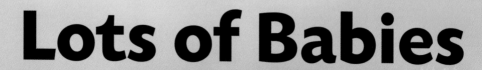

Lots of Babies

By late spring there are babies everywhere.

Lambs can stand soon after being born. Before long they are running and jumping.

A fawn stays close to its mother and drinks her milk.

Spring Fun

Many places have spring festivals to celebrate the end of winter and the start of new life.

Enjoy spring by planting seeds, spotting baby animals, or hanging up nesting boxes for birds.

A cherry blossom festival in Japan.

Did You Know...?

Every spring, gray whales leave warm Californian waters and swim all the way to Alaska in the far north.

When we have spring, it is fall in the southern half of the world.

At the Indian spring festival of Holi, people throw colored powder everywhere!

Hummingbirds lay the smallest eggs of all birds. Each egg is the size of a pea.

Useful Words

bud
A bump on a branch or stem. Leaves and flowers start as buds.

fawn
A baby deer.

spring
The time of year after winter and before summer.

sprout
To begin to grow above the ground.

Index